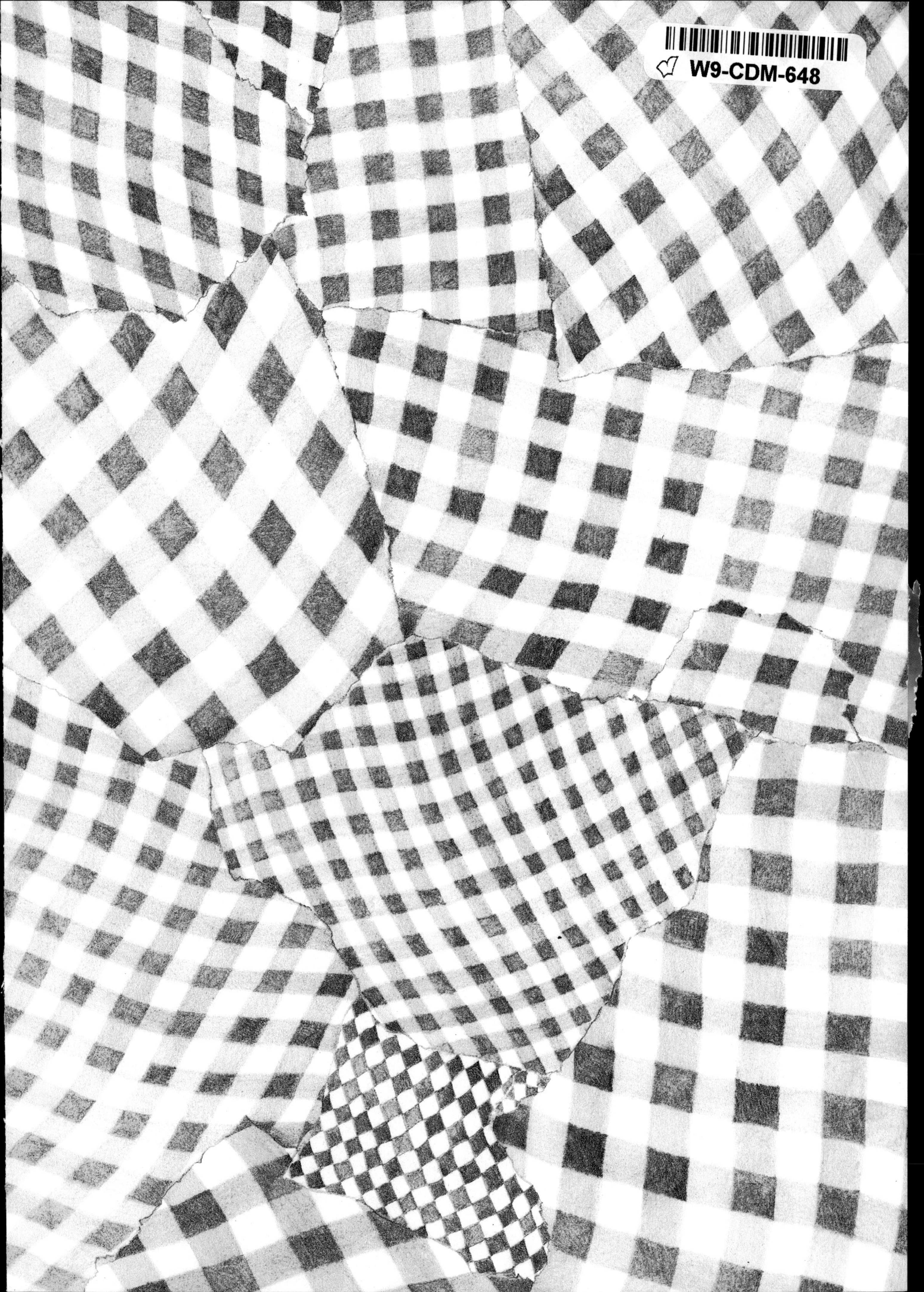

The Gingham Dog and the Calico Cat

THE
Gingham Dog
AND THE
Calico Cat

A POEM BY

Eugene Field

ILLUSTRATED BY

Johanna Westerman

North-South Books

NEW YORK · LONDON

For Jim and Mary Day

Published in the United States by North-South Books Inc., New York

Published simultaneously in Great Britain, Canada, Australia, and New Zealand
by North-South Books, an imprint of Nord-Süd Verlag AG,
Gossau Zürich, Switzerland.

Library of Congress Cataloging-in-Publication Data
Field, Eugene, 1850-1895. The gingham dog and the calico cat : a poem / by Eugene Field ;
illustrated by Johanna Westerman. 1. Toys—Juvenile poetry. 2. Children's poetry, American.
[1. Toys—Poetry. 2. Dogs—Poetry. 3. Cats—Poetry. 4. American poetry.]
I. Westerman, Johanna, ill. II. Title.
PS1667.G56 1994 811'.4—dc20 94-20049

A CIP record for this book is available from The British Library
ISBN 1-55858-291-6 (Trade binding)
ISBN 1-55858-292-4 (Library binding)

Designed by Marc Cheshire
1 3 5 7 9 TB 10 8 6 4 2
1 3 5 7 9 LB 10 8 6 4 2
Printed in Belgium

The Gingham Dog and the Calico Cat

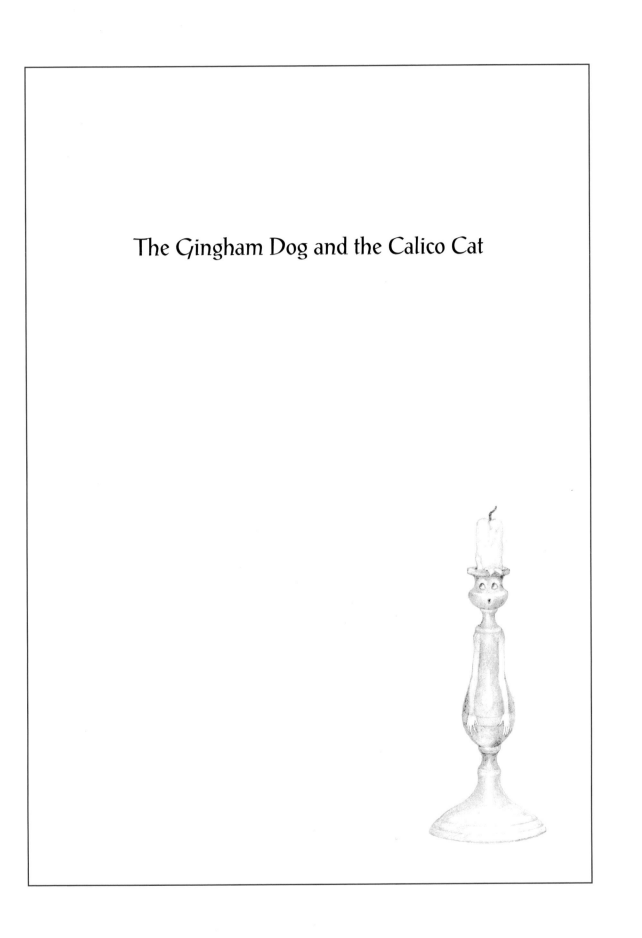

THE gingham dog and the calico cat
   Side by side on the table sat;
    'Twas half-past twelve, and (what do you think?)
Nor one nor t'other had slept a wink!

The old Dutch clock and the Chinese plate
Appeared to know as sure as fate
There was going to be a terrible spat.
(I wasn't there; I simply state
What was told me by the Chinese plate!)

The gingham dog went, "Bow-wow-wow!"

And the calico cat replied, "Mee-ow!"

The air was littered, an hour or so,
With bits of gingham and calico,

While the old Dutch clock in the chimney-place
Up with its hands before its face
For it always dreaded a family row!
(Now mind: I'm only telling you
What the old Dutch clock declares is true!)

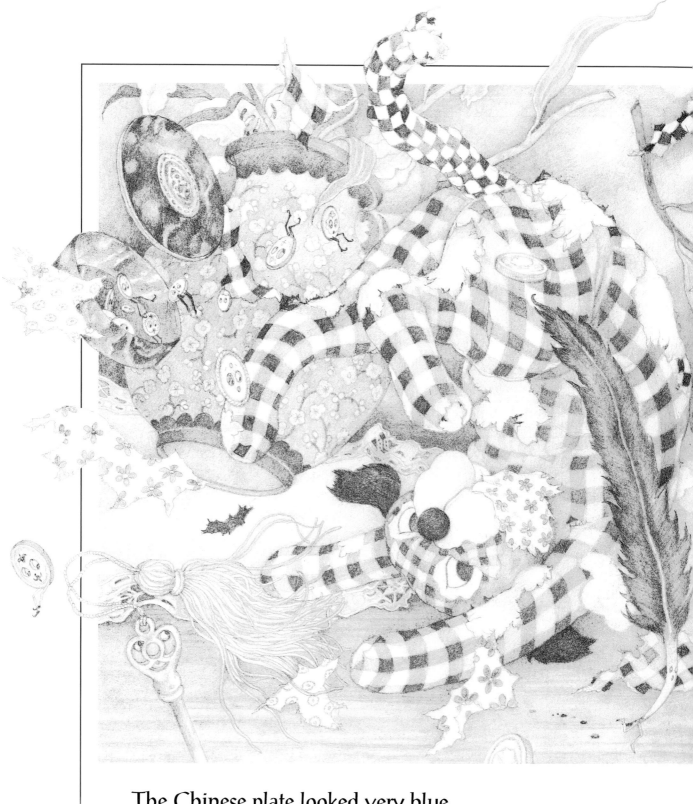

The Chinese plate looked very blue,
And wailed, "Oh dear! What shall we do?"

But the gingham dog and the calico cat
Wallowed this way and tumbled that,

Employing every tooth and claw
In the awfullest way you ever saw—
And, oh, how the gingham and calico flew!
    (Don't fancy I exaggerate—
    I got my news from the Chinese plate!)

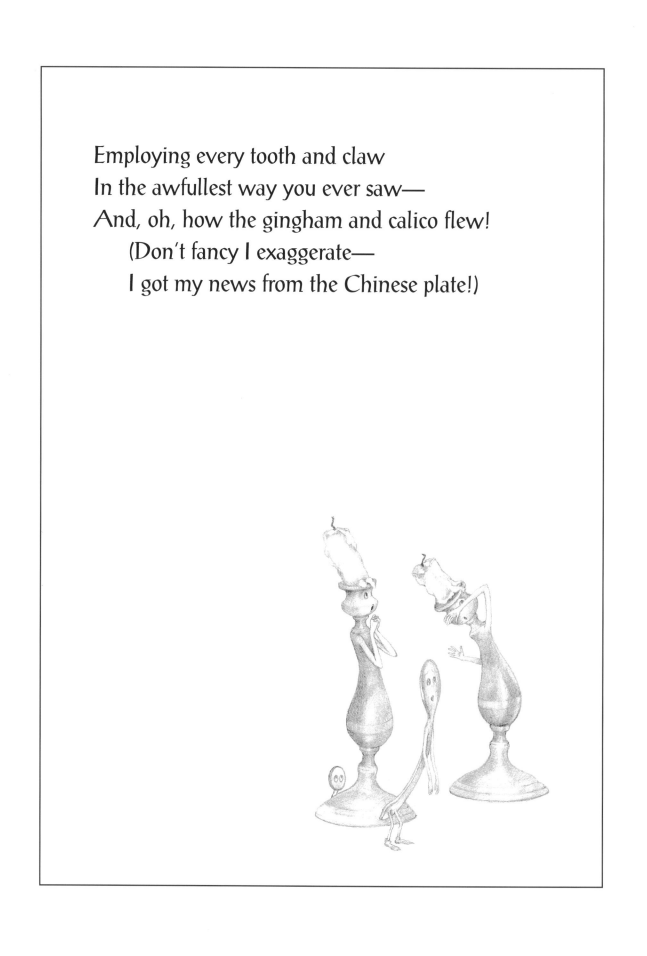

Next morning, where the two had sat

They found no trace of dog or cat;

And some folks think unto this day
That burglars stole that pair away!
 But the truth about that cat and pup
 Is this: They ate each other up!
Now what do you really think of that?

(The old Dutch clock, it told me so,
And that is how I came to know.)

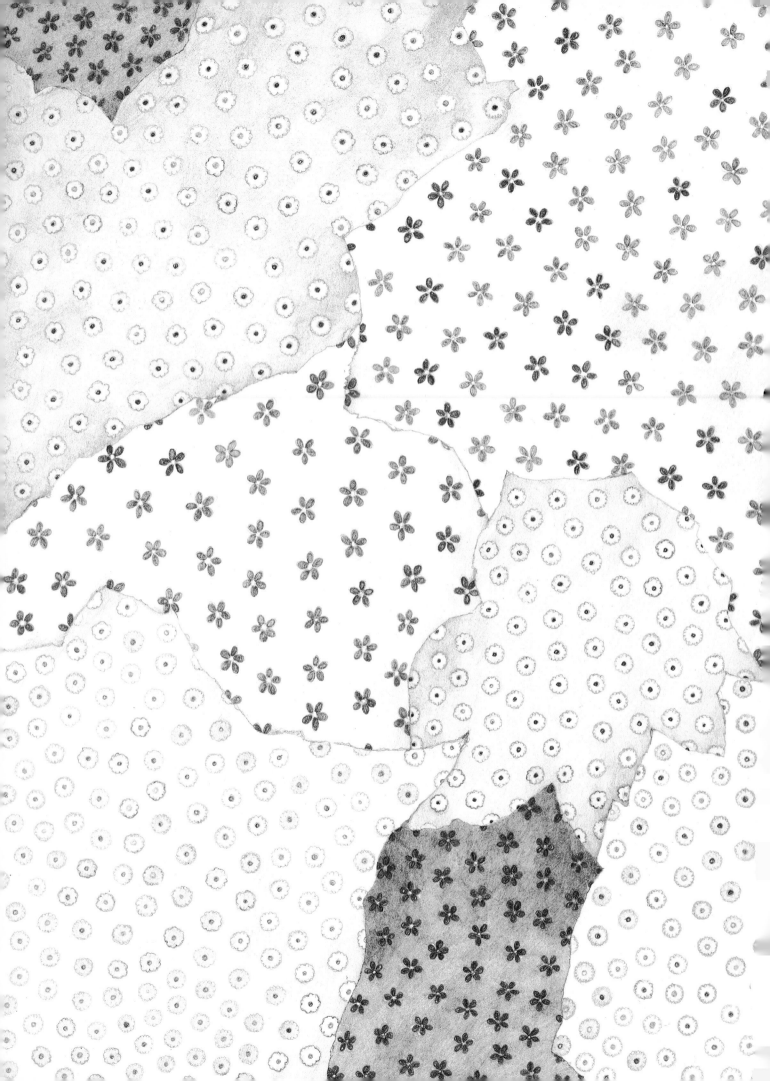